So You Want to Learn About

Reptiles & Amphibians

Written and Photographs by
Katrina Willoughby

© Willoughby Arts 2018

I hear you want to learn about reptiles and amphibians.

Reptiles and amphibians are cold blooded creatures that can be found in many regions of our world. Sometimes it is hard to tell them apart.

Both have skeletons, breathe with lungs, and most live near or in water. There are some differences between reptiles and amphibians.

When trying to decide if an animal is a reptile or an amphibian look for scales. Reptiles have scales. Amphibians do not.

The scales on this snake are easy to see. It is a reptile.

Some of the differences between reptiles and amphibians are easy to see and some are not.

Amphibian lungs aren't developed as well as reptiles. Air passes through an amphibian's skin to provide additional oxygen.

Many amphibians have gills early in life. Most amphibian's gills disappear as they get older, but a few keep their gills. This change is called metamorphosis. A good example of this is a tadpole that turns into a frog. Not all amphibians experience this.

Both reptiles and amphibians can lay eggs.

Above a painted turtle, a reptile, has dug a hole and is laying her eggs. Reptiles lay their eggs on land while amphibians start their lives in or very close to water. A few reptiles give birth to live babies.

For some lizards, turtles, tortoises, crocodiles and alligators the temperature that eggs are at while the babies are developing will determine if the babies that hatch are boys or girls.

A reptile that has legs will also have claws. Amphibians do not have claws.

This toad has toes, but doesn't have claws. It is an amphibian.

You can see the claws on this turtle's foot. It is a reptile.

Unlike you and me, reptiles and amphibians don't have ears. A thin flap of skin over the ear bone allows the vibrations caused by sound to enter their ear canal.

The word amphibious means lives on both land and in water. A gland helps keep amphibians moist by secreting mucus that keeps the skin wet. If they are away from water too long, they will dry up. When touched many amphibians feel wet.

A reptile, like the snake above, will have dry skin.

Reptiles include animals like lizards, turtles, tortoises, snakes, crocodiles and alligators.

Above you can see two reptiles!

There are three main types of amphibians: frogs and toads, salamanders and newts, and those without limbs called caecilians.

There are about 600 species of frogs and toads. The other types have less species. Caecilians don't have arms or legs and look a lot like snakes. Strong skulls let them dig into the dirt.

As adults, amphibians are carnivores. That means they eat only animals. They swallow their food whole. This lizard will have a hard time feasting on the cricket that is sitting on its head!

Most reptiles are also carnivores, but some turtles and lizards are omnivores or even herbivores. An omnivore eats both plants and animals while an herbivore eats only plants. Many reptiles can be seen ripping their food into pieces that they can swallow.

Snakes are reptiles that don't have legs. Some snakes can have over 300 pairs of ribs! Unlike you and me, the bones in a snake's skull are not all connected. Snakes can use muscles to open their mouths very large to swallow prey whole.

2/3 of snakes are not venomous and only 2 percent of all snakes are venomous to people.

Both snakes and lizards use their tongue to smell. They flick their tongue in and out to

collect scent particles. Scent particles are passed over a specialized part of their body called the Jacobson's organ.

Lizards have scales and claws. They are reptiles.

The Komodo dragon is the largest lizard. One is pictured below and on the last page.

The largest reptile is the saltwater crocodile. It can be over 12 feet long. Crocodiles and alligators are not lizards.

The largest amphibian is the Chinese Great Salamander which can grow to 6 feet long.

The picture to the left is from a much smaller salamander found in Texas. It is about 5 inches long.

The Cuban brown anole is an invasive species of lizard that is spreading across the southern United States. Invasive means that they didn't used to live in this area and their population is increasing. Their eggs were accidentally brought in when bag of soil where moved to this area.

Much of the southern United States has been home to the green anole. The brown anole is faster and stronger than the green anole. Now fewer green ones are seen. Both species eat primarily insects and the green anole can't compete with the strength of the brown ones.

Can you tell a frog from toad? Toads have bumpy skin while frog skin is smooth and often moist. It is more common for a toad to crawl while a frog is more likely to hop.

The top picture is a toad. The other picture is a frog.

Some reptiles have special 'tricks'. Crocodiles have a trick to allow them to dive deeper. They swallow rocks to make themselves heavier.

Some lizards have tails that will break off and wiggle to distract predators. The wiggling tail takes the attention of the predator while the lizard gets away. Their tail will grow back.

Alligators have very powerful tails. The tail can help propel them in and out of the water to get food.

While crocodiles are only found in saltwater, alligators live in fresh water or marshes that have brackish water.

Both crocodiles and alligators regrow teeth that break off. Thousands of teeth can be grown during their lives.

Have you heard of poison dart frogs? Some amphibians have glands that secrete poison. This makes them undesired by predators. If another animal tries to eat them it could get very sick. Poison dart frogs were used by ancient cultures by rubbing the tip of a weapon on the amphibian's skin. That would make the weapon even more dangerous.

Above you can see two different types of poison dart frogs!

You may see reptiles sunning themselves to warm.

The lizard above is camouflaged so that it can safely sun itself without predators easily seeing it.

Human's bodies create heat to keep them warm. This doesn't happen for reptiles and amphibians. They are cold blooded. Their body temperature changes with the weather around them. This is why reptiles like to sun themselves. They let the sun heat their bodies so they are warm enough to move.

This turtle is sunning itself on a log.

When it gets cold, you won't see reptiles and amphibians out walking around.

In winter both reptiles and amphibians hibernate. They slow their breathing and metabolism until they can pass through winter in a dormant, sleep like state.

Amphibians that hibernate need to be near water with a good oxygen supply so that they can absorb oxygen through their skin.

Some frogs will slow down so much that a heartbeat cannot be detected.

Frogs have a substance that acts like antifreeze to prevent their body from freezing. Ice crystals may form in other parts of their body like their bladder and under their skin.

This frog has camouflage that makes it blend in with its surroundings. Plants in the water look much like its skin, making it hard to see.

So….

Did you learn new things about reptiles and amphibians?

I hope you learned new things and enjoyed this book!

This is the third book in the series "So You Want to Learn About…" Please check out the other books in this series.

Thank you for reading.

Other books in this series

So You Want to Learn About Butterflies

So You Want to Learn About Turtles & Tortoises

So You Want to Learn About Insects & Bugs

www.ingramcontent.com/pod-product-compliance
Lightning Source LLC
Chambersburg PA
CBHW041756040426
42446CB00001B/60